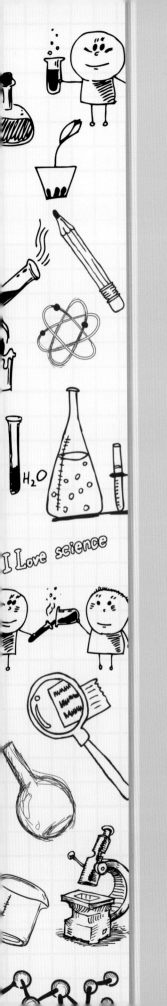

Learning Playground

Learning About Energy, Forces, and Motion

WORLD
BOOK

a Scott Fetzer company
Chicago

www.worldbookonline.com

World Book, Inc.
233 N. Michigan Avenue
Chicago, IL 60601
U.S.A.

For information about other World Book publications, visit our Web site at **http://www.worldbookonline.com** or call **1-800-WORLDBK (967-5325).**

For information about sales to schools and libraries, call **1-800-975-3250 (United States); 1-800-837-5365 (Canada).**

Library of Congress Cataloging-in-Publication Data

Learning about energy, forces, and motion.
    p. cm. -- (Learning playground)
    Summary: "An activity-based volume that introduces early-level physical science concepts, including energy and motion, different types of forces, and simple machines. Features include a glossary, an additional resource list, and an index"-- Provided by publisher.
    Includes index.
    ISBN 978-0-7166-0233-0
    1. Force and energy--Juvenile literature. 2. Motion--Juvenile literature. I. World Book, Inc.
    QC73.4.L43 2012
    531'.6--dc22
                            2011011521

Learning Playground
Set ISBN: 978-0-7166-0225-5

Printed in Malaysia by TWP Sdn Bhd, Johor Bahru
1st printing July 2011

Acknowledgments:
The publishers gratefully acknowledge the following sources for photography. All illustrations were prepared by WORLD BOOK unless otherwise noted.

Cover: Shutterstock, Dreamstime

Ashley Cooper pics/Alamy Images 12; blickwinkel/Alamy Images 4; Neil Cooper, Alamy Images 54; Corbis RF/Alamy Images 22; First Light/Alamy Images 16; imagebroker/Alamy Images 41; Image Source/Alamy Images 19; Leslie Garland Picture Library/Alamy Images 57; MIXA/Alamy Images 42; Richard Naude, Alamy Images 47; Alex Segre, Alamy Images 47; AP Photo 21; Dreamstime 4, 6, 10, 12, 22, 25, 30, 31, 33, 40, 42, 43, 46, 50, 51; LWA/Jay Newman/Getty Images 27; Martin Riedl, Taxi/Getty Images 24; iStockphoto 23, 56; B. & C. Alexander, Photo Researchers 26; Ellen B. Senisi, Photo Researchers 38; Shutterstock 4, 5, 6, 11, 13, 16, 17, 22, 23, 32, 36, 37, 40, 41, 51, 52, 53, 54, 55; WORLD BOOK photo 53.

Table of Contents

There is a glossary on page 62. Terms defined in the glossary are in type that **looks like this** on their first appearance on any spread (two facing pages).

What Is Energy?

Airplanes and other vehicles use energy from burning fuel to work.

Think of all the ways you move every day. You may run, play a sport, or walk to school. What gives you the power to move?

The answer is energy! Your body gets its energy from food. The energy you get makes the pushes and pulls that keep you moving.

← Pushing a wheelbarrow requires more energy than sitting at a desk.

Try this!

Energy can move from one object to another. Try this simple experiment to see how this happens. Line up some dominoes, as shown. Give one of the end dominoes energy by nudging it so that it tips over onto the domino next to it. Watch the energy pass from one domino to the next as they topple over.

Power plants generate electric energy.

Sailboats use energy from wind to move.

A car engine burns gasoline. As the gasoline burns, it gives off energy. That energy makes the pushes and pulls that turn the wheels.

Scientists define energy as "the ability to do work." Work doesn't just include things like taking out the trash. It can mean many other things, like throwing a ball or pushing a sled. Even sleep requires energy, so it is also a form of work.

There are many kinds of energy. Things that move, such as water and wind, have energy. Things that burn, such as fire, have energy. Even sound and light have energy.

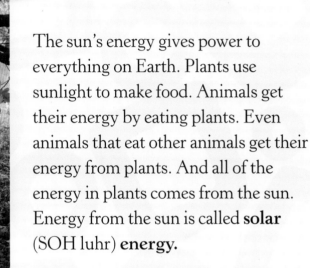

The sun's energy gives power to everything on Earth. Plants use sunlight to make food. Animals get their energy by eating plants. Even animals that eat other animals get their energy from plants. And all of the energy in plants comes from the sun. Energy from the sun is called **solar** (SOH luhr) **energy.**

Some buildings use solar energy to produce electric power. Devices called solar cells produce **electric current** directly from sunlight. The cells are grouped together on solar panels, which are often placed on roofs or other sunny places.

All plants and animals need energy from the sun to live.

Solar cells are grouped together on solar panels. They can make electric power directly from sunlight.

6

Solar cells provide power for spacecraft and satellites, handheld calculators, and wristwatches. They are also used to create electric power in places far from cities where there are no power lines.

Some buildings use solar energy to produce heat. A solar house has large windows that trap the sun's heat. The walls and floors absorb the heat during the day and release it at night. On cloudy days, people who live in a solar-heated home may use a wood-burning stove to provide heat.

Solar buildings may also use sunlight to heat water. These buildings have special collectors to capture the sun's heat. Usually the collectors are on the roof or on the sunniest side of the house. Liquid inside the collectors flows to a device called a heat exchanger in the basement. In the heat exchanger, heat from the fluid transfers to water that is stored in a tank for household use.

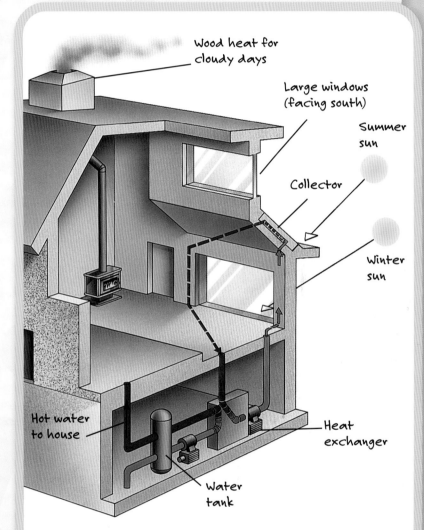

Wood heat for cloudy days

Large windows (facing south)

Summer sun

Collector

Winter sun

Hot water to house

Heat exchanger

Water tank

Energy from sunlight can be used to provide heat and hot water for buildings.

MAKE A SOLAR COLLECTOR

You can see how solar collectors work by making your own. Do this activity on a bright, sunny day.

MATERIALS

- Sheet of clear plastic or glass
- Water
- Thermometer
- Black baking tray, or one you can line with black plastic

DIRECTIONS

1. Fill the baking tray with cold water about ½ inch (1.25 centimeters) deep. Use the thermometer (tool for measuring temperature) to find out the water temperature. If you don't have one, test the water with your finger.

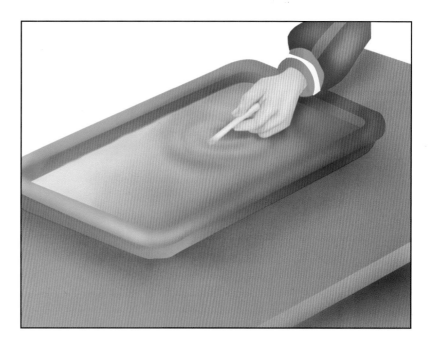

2. Place the glass or plastic over the tray. Leave the tray in the sunshine for an hour.

3. Take the lid off the tray and put the thermometer or your finger back into the water.

What has happened to the water temperature? How does it compare to the temperature of the air outside?

Energy from Wind

A push from the wind can make a kite fly. It can make a sailboat skim across the water. It can do other things, too. It can even pump water and light lamps.

People use wind energy to pump water for their homes. They do it with the help of a machine called a windmill. Windmills come in different shapes and sizes, but they are all alike in some ways.

Energy from wind helps to lift a kite into the air.

Windmills can be used to pump water or to grind grain.

Windmills are tall enough to catch the strong winds that blow high above the ground. They also have a wheel, which is the part that spins. The wheel has paddles, sails, or blades for the wind to push against. When the wind blows, the wheel spins. This makes a push that runs a water pump.

Turbines are similar to windmills, only they use wind to run an electricity-making machine called a **generator** (JEHN uh ray tuhr). There are even "wind farms," where many turbines make electricity for whole communities.

Of course, the wind doesn't always blow, so windmills and turbines don't always run. But water pumped by the windmill can be stored in tanks. And electricity made by turbines can be stored in batteries. People can use stored-up water and stored-up electricity in their homes.

Wind turbines convert wind energy into electric energy.

Energy from Burning

A candle is made of wax or a similar material that when melted gives off light.

You have seen candles burning. An orange flame dances around the wick, while the wax melts underneath and drips down. The candle gets shorter as the wax melts.

The candle wax has a kind of stored-up energy. It is a fuel. A fuel is something that provides energy to make light, heat, or a push that makes things move. Fuels are used to heat and cool buildings, cook food, power engines, and produce electric power. Most fuels are burned to release their energy.

Cars and other vehicles release exhaust as they burn fuel for energy.

The same thing happens to every fuel that is burned for energy. When it starts burning, the heat makes it break down and change to other things, such as ashes. As the fuel breaks down, it gives off energy. Some of the energy is light, and some is heat.

When gasoline is burned in a car engine, the heat energy makes the engine push. The push from the engine makes the car run.

The energy stored in fuels that are burned is called **chemical energy.**

Like all fuels, charcoal contains stored energy. It is used as a fuel to cook food on some grills.

As wood burns, it breaks down and turns into ash.

MAKE A SNAKE DANCER

Make this moving toy and you will see how heat energy can make something move.

MATERIALS

- Pencil
- Tracing paper
- Tape
- Construction paper
- Scissors
- Thimble
- Unsharpened pencil with eraser
- Spool
- Needle

DIRECTIONS

1. Trace the snake pattern shown on page 15 onto the tracing paper. Tape the paper onto the construction paper.

2. Cut around the outside of the shape. Then carefully poke your scissors through the center and cut out the circle. The hole should be big enough to fit over the thimble. If it is not, make it bigger. Then cut along the spiral line.

3. Push the thimble into the hole. Gently pull on the snake's head to make the spiral open up.

4. Stand the pencil in the spool, with the eraser up. If the pencil wobbles, stuff paper in the spool's hole. Have an adult help you poke the needle into the eraser. Hang the thimble over the needle, as shown on page 15, to make the snake "stand."

5. Put your snake dancer in a warm place—on a radiator, a fireplace mantel, or on top of a television set—or hold it over a lit light bulb.

What happens? The heat makes the air move, and the moving air makes the snake dancer spin around and around.

Energy from Electricity

Electricity is a kind of energy. When electricity flows through a wire, much as water flows through a hose, it is called an **electric current.** An electric current can do the same kind of work fuel can do. It can make light and heat. And it can make the push or pull that runs a machine.

Homes use electricity to power lights, kitchen appliances, and electronics.

Some commuter trains are powered by electricity that runs through wires connected to the top of the train.

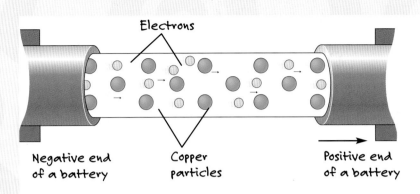

Electrons

Negative end
of a battery

Copper
particles

Positive end
of a battery

This illustration shows how electrons move through a copper wire that connects two ends of a battery. This movement is called an electric current.

When you turn on a light, ring a doorbell, or use a toaster, you start a parade. But it's a parade you can't see! It's a parade of tiny moving bits of matter called **electrons** (ih LEHK trahnz). Inside every electric wire, there are millions of electrons. When you press a button or turn a switch, electrons move through the wire. They make a strong push that gets work done. The energy of the moving electrons is called electricity. It makes lights and many household appliances work.

Electric cars are powered by rechargeable batteries.

IT'S ELECTRIC

Have you ever felt sparks fly when you pulled off your jacket? Or did you ever get a crackling shock when you touched a doorknob? These things happen because your body has been collecting electricity.

The sparks and crackles are called static (STAT ihk) electricity—**electrons** that pile up in one place. On cool, dry days, you scrape electrons loose from things. When you walk across a rug, or when your jacket rubs against you, the loose electrons stick to your body.

See the pull that electrons make by creating your own sticky balloon.

DIRECTIONS

1. Blow up a balloon, tie it shut, and tie a piece of string to it.

2. Rub the balloon with a wool cloth. Then touch the balloon to the cloth and let go of the string. What happens?

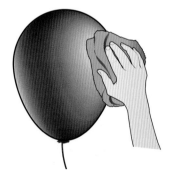

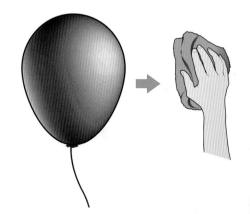

When you rub the balloon with the cloth, it picks up electrons from the cloth. The balloon then has more electrons than the cloth. When you put the balloon next to the cloth, the piled-up electrons on the balloon begin to move back to the cloth. They pull so hard that the balloon sticks to the cloth. That's static electricity!

You can see static electricity at work when you rub a balloon against your hair. This will cause your hair to stand up straight! Why do you think the hairs stick to the balloon but not to one another?

Energy from Atoms

All things—even you—are made up of billions and billions of "bits" that are smaller than anything you can imagine. These "bits" are called **atoms** (AT uhmz). Atoms are the tiniest parts that something can be broken into and still be the same stuff. For example, one atom of gold is the tiniest bit of gold possible.

Most atoms stay the same size. But sometimes a large atom shoots out a tiny piece from its nucleus (center). This type of atom is called a radioactive atom. The piece may strike the nucleus of a nearby atom. This atom may split and release more pieces, creating a chain reaction.

When a nucleus splits, it releases heat energy. This type of energy is called nuclear energy.

1. In some atoms, a nucleus may shoot out a small piece of itself.

A nuclear reactor is a machine that collects the heat from nuclear energy. The heat can be used to run **generators** that make electricity. Nuclear reactors also power many ships that stay at sea for long periods.

Rods of radioactive atoms heat pools of water. The heated water is used to run generators that create electricity.

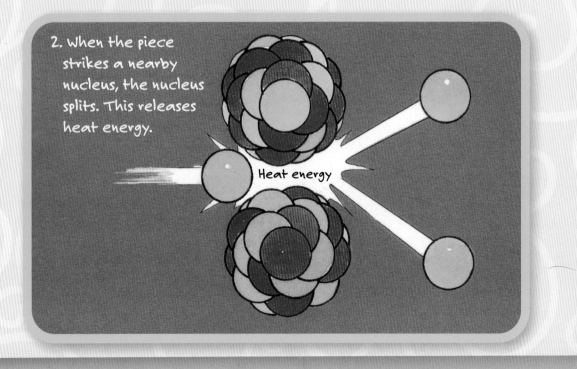

2. When the piece strikes a nearby nucleus, the nucleus splits. This releases heat energy.

Heat energy

WHAT MAKES IT WORK?

Find the kind of energy that makes each thing work.

1. A light bulb gets its energy from:
   a. burning wood
   b. electricity
   c. sunlight

2. An automobile is powered by:
   a. burning fuel
   b. wind
   c. a wheel

3. When you eat, your body gets energy:
   a. from the movement of your jaws when you chew
   b. from the food you eat
   c. from electric energy in your stomach

4. A sailboat uses the energy that comes from:
   a. light
   b. burning wood
   c. wind

5. A solar house gets energy from:
   a. candles
   b. sunlight
   c. steam

6. When you bake cookies in
   the oven, you use:
   a. heat energy
   b. the energy of moving things .
   c. moving water

When you push off a trampoline, you gain energy that lifts you high in the air.

Forces and Motion

Think of all the ways you can move about. You can walk, run, skip, or hop. You can also change direction. And you can pedal a bicycle or ride in a car to get from place to place. What do all of these actions have in common?

Each action is an example of motion. Motion is a change in position. An object moves if it starts at one place and ends up at another place.

At any given moment, every moving thing has a particular speed and moves in a particular direction. Speed and direction are the two parts of an object's motion.

As you may have guessed, energy causes objects to move. This energy is in the form of a **force**—a push or a pull. Forces change an object's motion.

You use the push of your legs to move a bicycle forward.

Forces push and pull all around us all the time. The wind blowing your hair pushes it with force. Magnets pull toward each other or push away from each other with forces. Gravity is also a force. For your entire life, Earth's gravity constantly pulls you down toward the ground.

Try this!

Build a small ramp using a binder or a book cover. Take an empty lidded plastic or tin can and roll it down the ramp by setting it on its side at the top of the ramp and letting it go. Note how far it rolls. Next, fill the can with rice or sand and roll it again. Did the empty can or the filled can roll farther? What happens if you fill the can with something heavier, like coins? How does weight affect the force of the can in motion?

Energy and Motion

Imagine you're on a sled at the top of a snowy hill. Your friend gives the sled one big push and—whoosh! You're soon speeding down the hill. How did your energy change?

When you are at the top of the hill, you have great **potential** (puh TEHN shuhl) **energy.** Potential energy is the energy that an object stores until it is used.

As you slide down the hill, you change your potential energy into **kinetic** (kih NEHT ihk) **energy.** Kinetic energy is the energy of motion.

A moving sled has lots of kinetic energy.

There are different kinds of potential energy. Coal has potential energy in the form of **chemical energy.** That energy is stored inside the tiny **atoms** that make up coal. A coal-burning power plant can convert this stored chemical energy to electric energy.

When you wind up a clock, potential energy becomes stored in the clock's spring. As the hands of the clock move, this energy changes into the kinetic energy that allows the clock to work.

A child on a swing shows how potential (stored) energy can become kinetic (moving) energy. In the top illustration, the girl has kicked herself back from position A to position B. While hanging in position B, she has a lot of potential energy but no kinetic energy. In the bottom illustration, the girl is swinging from position B to position D. While moving through position C, she has a lot of kinetic energy but no potential energy.

MAKE A SPOOL ENGINE

Find out how a spool engine uses a twisted rubber band to store potential energy.

MATERIALS

- Circular slice of a candle about 1.25 inches (3 centimeters) across, with a hole in the center (To slice the candle, use a dinner knife that has been held under very hot water.)

- Rubber band

- 2 toothpicks

- Empty spool

DIRECTIONS

1. Push the rubber band through the center of the spool. Break one of the toothpicks in half and push one half through the loop of the rubber band at one end of the spool.

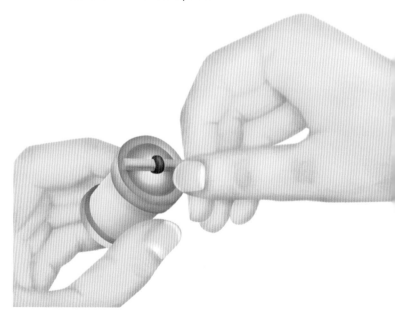

2. Push the other end of the
   rubber band through the
   hole in the candle.

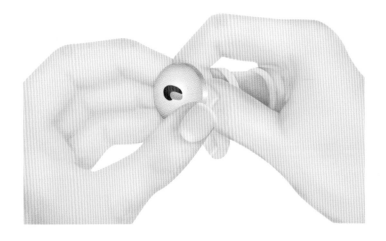

3. Push the second
   toothpick through the
   loop of the rubber band
   at the candle end.
   Wind up the engine very
   tightly by turning this
   toothpick.

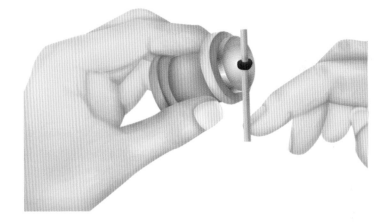

4. Place the engine on the
   floor. Describe what
   happens using the terms
   potential energy and
   kinetic energy.

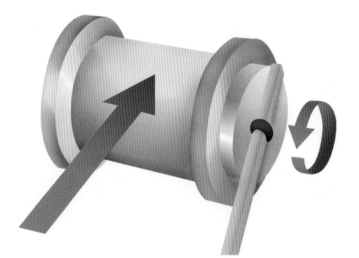

The Invisible Push

The light turns green, and the car starts to move quickly. You feel as if a big, invisible hand pushes you back in the car seat. When the car stops quickly, the same "hand" seems to push you forward.

What is this invisible "something" that pushes you when a car starts and stops? It's a **force** called **inertia** (ihn UHR shuh).

Because of inertia, an object in motion will stay in motion until a force acts on it.

Try this!

Try this activity to see inertia at work. On a smooth tabletop or other flat surface, stack three or more pennies on top of a nickel. Then set a quarter about 5 inches (12.5 centimeters) away from the stack. With one fingertip, flick the quarter strongly toward the nickel. With enough practice, you can make the quarter strike the nickel with the right amount of energy, so that the quarter stops moving when it makes contact and the nickel slides out from under the pennies. The pennies have not been touched, so they have no energy to move sideways. Instead, gravity pulls them straight down. Is it necessary to have the thicker nickel at the base of the coin tower instead of a coin the same size as those above it? Why?

Inertia describes the way things resist a change in movement. When something is stopped, it stays stopped. It starts to move only when a force—a push or a pull—makes it move. And when something is moving, it tends to keep moving. It won't stop until another force stops it.

When a car starts to move, your body tries to stay stopped. So you feel yourself pressing back as the car seat moves forward. And when the car stops, your body tends to keep moving. Inertia "pushes" you forward. Your seat belt is there to hold you back.

You can feel inertia when your body moves forward as a car quickly comes to a stop.

A Force for Stopping

Creating friction between the skateboard and the pavement helps a skateboarder to stop.

There's a big stick on the sidewalk. Slow down your bike! Then you can go around the stick safely.

Your bike has brakes to help it stop. When you squeeze the **levers** on the handlebars or push the pedals backward with your feet, the brakes rub against the wheels and stop them from turning. The rubbing that stops the wheels is called **friction** (FRIHK shuhn).

Friction happens because all things have a rough surface. Even things that look shiny and polished have very tiny areas that are not smooth. When one object slides across another, the rough spots rub against one another. This rubbing, or friction, makes things move more and more slowly, until finally they stop.

Friction is useful when it helps you stop your bike. But sometimes we want things to keep moving smoothly. Then we need to lessen friction. We can do this with a slippery substance, such as oil or grease. For example, the grease on your bicycle chain lessens friction so that you can pedal easily and smoothly.

There are many ways that we use friction for safety and control. People who build roads also help tires keep their grip. They cover roads with a rough surface made of sand, gravel, asphalt, and cement. In both dry and wet conditions, this surface produces friction with tires.

Mechanical brakes are commonly used on bicycles. When the rider squeezes a lever on the handlebar, two brake levers press rubber brake pads against the wheel rim. This slows the wheel.

Brake off

Brake on

Cable to lever on handlebar

Brake levers

Tire

Brake pads

Wheel rim

WORKING WITH FRICTION

One way we can reduce **friction** is by using ball bearings. The moving parts are kept apart with balls that roll smoothly. But sometimes we need to create friction to slow down or stop. Try these activities to see how friction works.

MATERIALS

- 2 cans that fit together, one on top of the other (cans should be full, not empty)
- Marbles

Reducing Friction

1. Place one can on top of the other. Try to spin the top one around.

2. Now put a handful of marbles between the top can and the bottom can. Does the top can spin around? Explain.

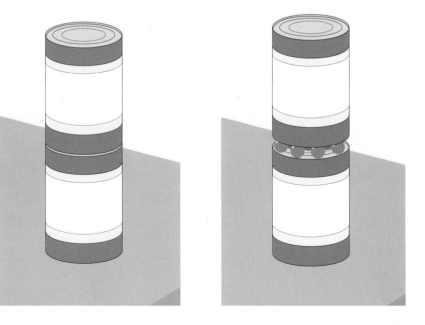

Causing Friction

1. Place the heavy book on a smooth floor or table. Attach the rubber band to the string and tie the string around the book. Pull the rubber band to move the book. Measure the length of the rubber band when the book first begins to move. This length shows the work needed to overcome the friction.

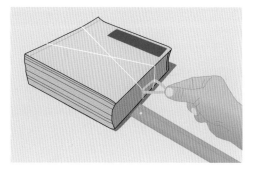

MATERIALS

- Heavy book (a phone book works well)
- Rubber band
- String, about 36 inches (about 1 meter) long
- Ruler or tape
- 4 juice cans, each 6 ounces (150 milliliters)
- Pen or pencil
- Paper

2. Place the cans on their sides under the book. Pull the rubber band again. Measure the length of the rubber band when the book first moves. Did it take more or less work to move the book?

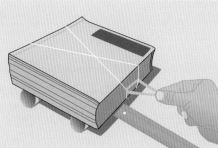

3. Try the experiment again and again. You could use a lighter or heavier book, or smaller or larger rollers, such as pens or larger cans. You could alo try using rubber bands of different sizes or a book with a smoother or rougher cover. These variables may change the results of your experiment.

4. Write down your results and observations. Does the rubber band stretch more when the book lies flat or when it rolls on cans? Which variables made it harder to pull the book? Which ones reduced the friction and made it easier? Keep testing your conclusions.

A Downward Pull

Gravity is perhaps the most obvious kind of **force** on Earth. The planet's gravity constantly pulls you toward the ground. Without gravity, you could jump into the air and keep moving into outer space!

The force of gravity pulls on all objects, big and small. For example, Earth's gravity pulls the moon. But the moon's gravity also pulls Earth.

Your body also has gravity. It pulls Earth toward you. But Earth is trillions of times heavier than you. There's no way you could win a tug of war with Earth, so Earth stays put while you get pulled down to the ground.

Gravity and **friction** work together to change an object's motion. These forces pull a rolling ball to a stop. If the ball were moving in the emptiness of space, it would keep on moving with the same speed and direction.

How do airplane wings affect the pull of gravity? They have a special teardrop shape, called an airfoil, which cuts the air in a way that lifts the plane into the air. Make an airfoil by folding a thick piece of paper in half without creasing it so that the folded side is still rounded.

Tape the loose ends of the paper together. Next, tape two pieces of string, each about 1 ½ feet (45 centimeters) long, to each end of the rounded edge of the paper. Ask an adult to dangle the airfoil in front of a box fan with the rounded edge facing the fan. Try to get the airfoil to lift on its own by adjusting the fan speed and the shape of the airfoil. Which shape works best?

Try this!

No matter how hard you kick a ball, gravity will always cause it to fall back to the ground.

Balanced Forces

When forces are balanced, the two equal pushes or pulls cancel each other out.

Imagine a restaurant with a swinging door leading to the kitchen. Two servers try to push the door open from opposite sides at the same time. One holds a huge bowl of spaghetti. The other balances a tray of dishes. If they both push with the same **force**, the door doesn't move. But if the server with the spaghetti does not push as hard as the other server, the door swings open. And crash—spaghetti flies everywhere!

When equal forces push or pull on an object from opposite sides, that object is in equilibrium (ee kwuh LIHB ree uhm). An object in equilibrium is balanced. It won't move or tip over unless an extra push or pull is added from one direction.

Gravity pulls all objects downward, toward the center of Earth. Every object has its own center of gravity, the spot where it can be balanced. An object balanced at its center of gravity will be in equilibrium.

Try this!

Ask an adult to help you carefully stick a small fork into a small potato, with the top side of the fork facing upward. Next, find a pencil that is longer than the fork. Push the pencil into the other side of the potato until about 1 inch (2.5 centimeters) sticks out above the fork. Balance the pencil tip on the edge of a table, with the fork extending below the table. The potato stays balanced because the system's center of gravity is actually in the pencil tip!

Machines can be as small and simple as a needle used for sewing.

Making Work Easier

As you have learned, scientists define energy as the ability to do work. Whenever we use energy, we do work. But some forms of work are harder than others. Lifting a piece of paper is easy work. It takes little energy. But lifting a piece of furniture is much harder.

People have invented machines to make certain kinds of work easier. Machines can be any shape and size, but they all have one thing in common: they help people do work.

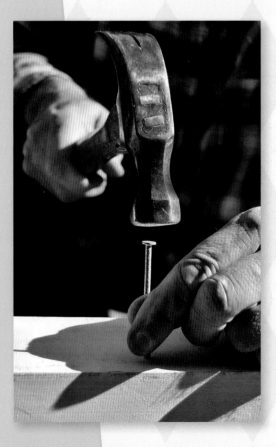

A hammer is an example of a simple machine. It makes it easier to pound nails into walls and boards.

A bottle opener is a simple machine. It is a lever that makes prying the lid off bottles easier.

When we think of machines, we usually think of big ones with many parts. These machines do big jobs, such as digging holes, washing clothes, or mowing lawns. But some machines are small. You cut things out with a small machine—a pair of scissors. You sew with a small machine—a needle and thread. And you tighten a **screw** with a small machine—a screwdriver. These small machines help you do work, too.

Simple machines are basic tools that change the way **force** is used to do work. There are six types of simple machines: the **inclined plane,** the **lever,** the **pulley,** the screw, the **wedge,** and the **wheel and axle.** They can be combined to make bigger machines. All machines, even ones as complex as automobiles, are based in some way on simple machines.

A forklift is a machine that helps to lift heavy loads.

What Are Levers?

Can you lift your best friend higher than your head? Can your best friend lift you? It doesn't sound easy, but it is. When you and your friend play on a seesaw, that's exactly what you are doing.

The seesaw you and your friend are riding is really a kind of **simple machine** called a **lever** (LEHV uhr). A lever makes pushing and lifting easy, even when things are hard to move.

People use crowbars to pry things loose.

A seesaw is a kind of lever. The two arms of the lever balance on the fulcrum at the center.

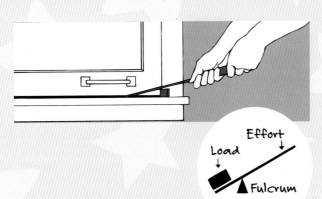

The lever is one of the earliest and simplest machines. It has a short distance between the fulcrum and load, and a long distance between the fulcrum and the point where effort is applied.

The simplest kind of lever is a straight stick or board and something to rest it on. Suppose you want to move something heavy—a big rock, for example. You can push one end of a strong board under the rock. Then you can rest the middle of the board on a log. This is the resting place, or **fulcrum** (FUHL kruhm). The end of the board near you sticks up. If you push down on the high end of the board, the other end will move up. The heavy rock will move, too.

When you ride a seesaw, you and your friend take turns using it as a lever. The middle of the seesaw is the fulcrum. Your weight pushes one end down and lifts your friend up. Then your friend's weight pushes the other end down and lifts you up.

A nutcracker consists of two bars that are attached at a hinge. You squeeze the bars to put pressure on the nut, which causes its shell to break open.

MAKE A LEVER

Levers make it easier to lift big, heavy things. They can also help you pick up things you can't quite reach. This alligator long-arm uses pairs of levers to make other levers move.

DIRECTIONS

1. Use the ruler and pencil to mark out six strips of corrugated cardboard. Each strip should be about 7 inches (18 centimeters) long and 1 inch (2.5 centimeters) wide. Leave a "tooth" on two of the strips, as shown.

2. Cut out the strips. Then use the pencil to punch a hole in the middle of each one.

3. Fasten together the pairs of strips without teeth to make two X shapes.

4. Use the patterns at the bottom of page 45 to cut the alligator's top and bottom jaws out of the green construction paper and its teeth out of the white paper. Draw two rows of teeth on the white paper.

5. Glue the teeth onto the alligator's top and bottom jaws along the dotted line, as shown. Draw in the eyes and nose.

MATERIALS

- Corrugated cardboard
- Ruler
- Pencil
- Scissors
- 7 paper fasteners
- Green and white construction paper
- Glue

6. Fasten the last two strips of cardboard so that the teeth face each other.

7. Glue the alligator's bottom jaw onto the bottom cardboard strip. Glue the alligator's top jaw to the other cardboard strip.

8. Line up the cardboard X shapes as shown above right, and punch the rest of the holes. Fasten the shapes together.

Your alligator long-arm works like a pair of scissors. When you close the handles together, the end with teeth closes, too. You and your friends can take turns using the long-arm to pick up small cardboard fish or "pirate treasure." See who can make the biggest catch!

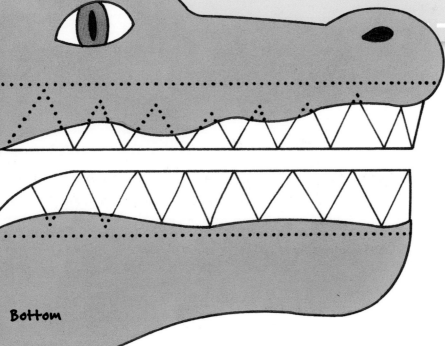

Top

Bottom

What Are Inclined Planes?

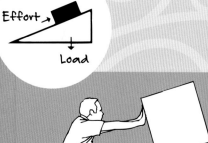

Effort

Load

The inclined plane makes it easier to slide or skid a load upward than to lift it directly.

Is a slanted board a machine? It is if you use it to do work. It is a kind of **simple machine** called an **inclined plane** (ihn KLYND playn). *Inclined* means slanted, and a plane is a flat surface. So an inclined plane is a flat surface that slants, like a slide on a playground.

An inclined plane makes it easy to move things up and down. When you use an inclined plane, you spread out the amount of work you do. If you lift a heavy box onto a table, you move it only a short distance—straight up. But you are doing all the lifting at once. If you slide the box up an inclined plane, you do the lifting little by little, so the job is easier.

There are other ways to use inclined planes, too. When you wheel your bike or roll a wheelchair up and down a ramp, you are using an inclined plane.

Escalators are moving inclined planes that help transport people up stairs.

The kind of inclined plane you use most often may not look like one. A stairway is an inclined plane with steps on it. The steps help keep the incline walkable by giving your feet something to grab onto. Without the steps you might slide right off! Imagine how long the inclined plane would have to be if you flattened out the stairs!

People use ramps instead of stairs to move wheelchairs into elevated spaces.

Activity

MAKE AN INCLINED PLANE

An **inclined plane** makes work easier by requiring less **force** to move an object. This simple experiment shows you how!

MATERIALS

- Thick rubber band
- Small stack of books
- Coffee mug, or other cup with a handle
- Ruler

DIRECTIONS

1. Cut the rubber band and tie one end to the handle of the coffee mug. Tie a tight double knot so it doesn't come loose!

2. On a sturdy table, build an inclined plane by leaning one book at an angle against a stack of books. The stack should be 3 to 4 inches (7.5 to 10 centimeters) high.

3. Move the coffee mug from the table to the top of the stack of books by holding the opposite end of the rubber band and gently lifting the mug straight up in the air. Just before setting the mug down on the stack, measure the length of the rubber band.

4. Return the coffee mug to the table. Turn the mug on its side. Drag it up the inclined plane from the table to the top of the stack of books by pulling it with the rubber band. Measure the length of the rubber band just before you reach the top of the stack of books.

5. Compare the two measurements. Which way of moving the mug stretched the rubber band farther? (The longer the rubber band, the more force is needed to move the mug.) Did the mug feel heavier when the rubber band was stretched longer?

6. Lower the inclined plane by removing a book from the stack. Try dragging the mug up the inclined plane again. Is the rubber band longer or shorter than before? What if you raise the inclined plane by adding books to the stack? You can also try this experiment with different objects to find out if the rubber band acts the same way for other weights.

A knife is a sharp, thin wedge used for cutting.

What Are Wedges?

Be careful! That knife is sharp! Don't stick yourself with that pushpin! Working with sharp things means taking special care. But some things have to be sharp to work well. A dull knife or a pushpin without a point isn't much help at all.

Sharp things have a special shape that makes work easier. They are really all one kind of machine—a machine called a **wedge** (wehj). The thin, sharp end of a wedge can cut or push into things easily. Then the thicker part of the wedge can push through.

Effort
Load   Load

The wedge, when struck with a mallet or hammer, exerts a large **force** on its sides.

Pruning shears are two sharp wedges joined together. Shears and other scissors are also considered levers.

Knives, saws, and scissors are wedges for cutting. Pushpins, nails, and needles are wedges used for pushing into or through things. The point makes it easy for the pushpin to stick into a bulletin board, for the nail to push into wood, and for the needle to push through cloth.

Axes and metal wedges are used to push the sharp edge into a log. Then the wider part spreads the wood and makes it split.

Many boats have a wedge-shaped bow, or front end. The bow cuts through the water and makes it easy for the boat to glide along.

Boats have wedge-shaped bows to help them glide through the water.

When rotated, screws can be made to move into, or out of, an object.

Wham! Wham! Wham! It is easy to nail two pieces of wood together. You just pound in nails with a hammer. But fastening two pieces of wood together with a **screw** is not so easy. The screw has to be turned many times to go into the wood.

A screw has a winding edge called a thread. The thread usually goes from the bottom nearly all the way to the top. When you turn the screw, you wind the thread into the wood.

Load

Effort

← The jackscrew is a combination of the **lever** and the screw. It can lift a heavy load with small effort.

X

Turning a screw takes more time than pounding in a nail the same size. But the winding thread of the screw is much longer than the straight sides of the nail. There is more of it to grip and hold the wood. So for some jobs, a screw works better than a nail. It holds things together better than nails.

Try this!

A light bulb has a screw at the bottom so it can be securely fastened inside a lamp socket.

A screw is really an **inclined plane** that curves around and around. Make a paper screw and see for yourself. Cut a triangle shape, as shown at the bottom of these pages, from a corner of construction paper. Mark the square corner with an X.

The long cut edge is an inclined plane. Color this edge with a crayon or marker. Starting at the straight end, with the X next to the eraser, wind the triangle around a pencil. The colored edge shows you how the inclined plane winds around the screw to form the threads.

What Are Wheels and Axles?

Four wheels, two axles (AKS uhlz), a box, and a handle. That is all a wagon is. But with a wagon, you can easily carry a couple of friends or even give your dog a ride.

When you use a wagon, **wheels and axles** are helping you. You can see the wheels. They are the round parts that roll over the ground. The axles are the rods that connect each pair of wheels. The wheels and axles turn together.

A wheel and axle can transport heavy loads with little effort on the part of a person.

A windlass is a kind of wheel and axle used to lift weights and pull loads. In this photograph, women use a windlass to bring up water from a well.

The wheel and axle above has a rope attached to the axle to lift the load. The crank handle is the point where effort is applied.

A skateboard has two pairs of wheels on fixed axles.

Putting wheels and axles on something makes it easier to move. It would be hard to pull a wagon without wheels. It would just drag over the ground. But wheels on axles roll along smoothly. Cars, trucks, and buses have wheel-and-axle parts, too.

Every day you are helped by other kinds of wheels—wheels that do not roll. A doorknob is a kind of wheel-and-axle machine. The knob is the wheel! You turn it to make the axle pull back the latch so the door can open.

A pencil sharpener has a wheel and axle, too. The handle is part of a wheel. When you turn the handle, it turns an axle that makes the other parts work.

What Are Pulleys?

Suppose someone asked you to lift a hippopotamus! It sounds impossible, but with a **simple machine** called a **pulley** (PUL ee), you could do it.

A pulley is a special kind of **wheel and axle.** A rope or steel cable fits around the rim of the wheel. When one end of the rope is pulled down, the rope slides over the wheel, which turns on the axle. Then the load at the other end moves up.

With one pulley, the load moves up as far as you pull the rope down. You work just as hard to pull the rope as you would to pick up the load, but you can pull in a direction that is easier for you.

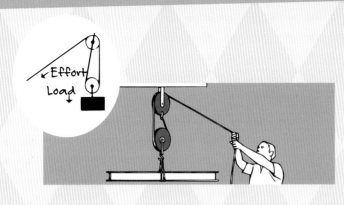

Effort
Load

The pulley consists of a wheel with a grooved rim over which a rope is passed. It is used to change the direction of the effort applied to the rope. A block and tackle uses two or more pulleys to reduce the amount of effort needed to lift a load.

With two pulleys, you can make lifting even easier. The second pulley is attached to the thing you lift. Each part of the rope between the pulleys holds half the weight, so you pull only half as hard to move the load. But the load is held up by twice as much rope. So you will have to pull the rope twice as far as the distance you want the load to move.

The more pulleys you use, the easier it is to lift a load. But you will have to pull more and more rope. You might be able to lift that hippopotamus with a hundred pulleys, but you will have to pull a lot of rope!

Pulleys make it easier to lift heavy objects, such as boats.

MAKE A COMPLEX MACHINE

Simple machines are often combined to make even more useful machines. Make your own complex machine that uses a **lever** and a **pulley** to pick up small objects.

MATERIALS

- Small cardboard box
- Thread spool
- Scissors
- Thick cardboard
- Paper fasteners
- Cotton thread
- Hook or magnet
- Wire
- Cork

Optional items (for making decorative wheels):

- 3 knitting needles
- 6 thread spools
- Modeling clay

DIRECTIONS

To Make the Arm:

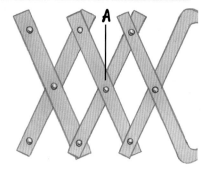

Note: you can skip this part of the activity if you made the lever arms from the activity on pages 44-45.

1. Cut six strips from a thick sheet of cardboard. The strips should be 7 inches (18 centimeters) long and 1 inch (2.5 centimeters) wide. Cut two curves at the ends of two of them.

2. Lay the strips in a crisscross pattern and join them with paper fasteners, as shown above. Use one large paper fastener (A) in the middle to attach the arm to the body.

To Make the Pulley:

1. Cut a hole in the back of the box big enough to fit in a thread spool. Wind thread around a spool, and tie a hook on the end.

2. Push the wire through one side of the box. Slide the thread spool onto the wire. Push the wire out the other side.

3. Bend the wire to make a handle.

4. Push some wire through the cork. Bend the wire at either side to make "legs," as shown to the right. Tape this to the front of the box.

5. Pull the thread over the cork, with the hook hanging down, as shown at the bottom of this page.

To Make the Wheels (Optional):

1. If you'd like to decorate your machine, you can make caterpillar wheels and tracks. Push the knitting needles through the ends and the middle of the base of the box. Slide a thread spool or film container onto both ends of each needle. Secure the ends with a lump of modeling clay.

2. To make a caterpillar track, cut two strips of corrugated cardboard. They should be long enough to wind over all three sets of wheels. Use adhesive tape to join the ends of the track together.

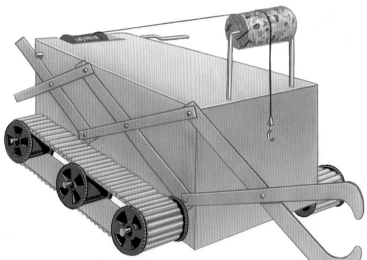

Experiment with your machine. Collect as many objects as you can. How many of these objects can you pick up with your model? What can you pick up with the pulley and hook? What can you pick up with the stretching arm?

IDENTIFY SIMPLE MACHINES

The people in the picture are all using different kinds of **simple machines**. Can you find the machine that each riddle below is describing?

1. **Wheels and axles** make me go. I use a **wedge** to scrape up snow.

2. I'm pretty clever—I dig with a **lever.** My teeth are wedges with pointed edges.

3. With a **screw** and handle, I'm strong. I'll prove it. I can lift a house if you want me to move it.

4. Moving wedges with very sharp edges will help you prune and trim your hedges.

5. Don't want to climb? Take a ride on me. I'm an **inclined plane** with steps, you see.

6. You'll find me where kids swing, climb, and run. I'm an inclined plane that you ride for fun.

7. **Pulleys** raise me to let in sun, or lower me when the day is done.

8. What are you riding? Wheels for the street—and small wheels with levers you work with your feet.

Glossary

atom one of the tiny particles, or bits, that all matter is made of. Most materials are made up of atoms from many different elements. But each chemical element consists of atoms of one basic type.

chemical energy the energy stored in a fuel.

electric current electricity that flows through a wire.

electron a tiny part of an atom that whirls around the atom's center, or nucleus.

force a push or a pull.

friction the rubbing of one object or kind of matter against another. Friction makes things move more and more slowly, until they stop.

fulcrum the support on which a lever turns or is supported in moving or lifting something.

generator a machine that changes mechanical energy into electric energy.

inclined plane a simple machine shaped like a ramp.

inertia the tendency of objects to stay either at rest or in motion.

kinetic energy the energy of motion.

lever a simple machine made of a long object that rests and turns on a fulcrum (pivot).

potential energy the energy that an object stores until it is used.

pulley a simple machine made of a rope or chain wrapped around a wheel.

screw a simple machine shaped like a ramp wrapped around a central shaft.

simple machine any of six basic tools that change the way force is used to do work.

solar energy energy from the sun.

wedge a simple machine with a thin, sharp edge that can cut or push into things easily.

wheel and axle a simple machine with a wheel attached to a thin axle (shaft).

Find Out More

Books

Energy Is Everywhere by June Young (Children's Press, 2006)

Energy Makes Things Happen by Kimberly Brubaker Bradley and Paul Meisel (HarperCollins, 2003)

Experiments with Motion by Salvatore Tocci (Children's Press, 2003)

Forces Make Things Move by Kimberly Brubaker Bradley and Paul Meisel (HarperCollins, 2005)

Levers by Valerie Bodden (Creative Education, 2011)

Move It! Motion, Forces and You by Adrienne Mason and Claudia Dávila (Kids Can Press, 2005)

Pulleys by Valerie Bodden (Creative Education, 2011)

Websites

Amusement Park Physics
http://www.learner.org/interactives/parkphysics/
A series of amusement park rides demonstrates the different ways that forces act on people and objects.

EcoKids: Get Energy-Wise
http://www.ecokids.ca/pub/eco_info/topics/energy/intro/index.cfm
Learn about what energy is and how our use of energy affects the planet.

Edheads: Simple Machines
http://www.edheads.org/activities/simple-machines/index.htm
The games on this interactive site explore the different types of simple and compound machines we use every day.

Energy Quest
http://energyquest.ca.gov/index.html
At Energy Quest, movies, games, stories, and fact sheets teach the basics of energy—where it comes from, how it works, and how we use it.

Inventor's Toolbox
http://www.mos.org/sln/Leonardo/InventorsToolbox.html
Explore simple machines—and the ways in which they combine to make more complex machines—at this educational site from the Museum of Science in Boston.

Little Shop of Physics
http://littleshop.physics.colostate.edu/amazingphysics.htm
At this website you will find experiments in force, energy, and motion, along with other basic physics concepts.

Science Snacks: Snacks About Mechanics
http://www.exploratorium.edu/snacks/iconmechanics.html
Quick and easy experiments turn everyday objects into physics lessons at this website.

Index

Activities